Mrs. Goddard

Senior Editor Jane Yorke
Art Editor Toni Rann
Editorial Director Sue Unstead
Art Director Colin Walton
Photography Stephen Oliver
Additional photography Jane Burton,
Peter Chadwick, Philip Dowell,
Michael Dunning, Colin Keates
Series Consultant Neil Morris

This is a Dorling Kindersley Book
published by Random House, Inc.

First American edition, 1990

Library of Congress Cataloging-in-Publication Data
My first look at seasons.
     p. cm.
   Summary: Photographs depict the seasons and their highlights.
   ISBN 0-679-80621-0
   1. Seasons – Pictorial works – Juvenile works. [1. Seasons.]
   I. Random House (Firm)
   QB637.4. M9 1990
   508 – dc20
   89-63094 CIP AC

Manufactured in Italy 1 2 3 4 5 6 7 8 9 10

Phototypeset by Flairplan Phototypesetting Ltd, Ware, Hertfordshire
Reproduced in Hong Kong by Bright Arts
Printed in Italy by L.E.G.O.

·MY · FIRST · LOOK · AT ·

Seasons

Random House New York

Spring

In the spring baby animals are born.

bird's
nest

umbrella

lamb

tulips

buds

raincoat

flowers

chicks

Easter
eggs

Spring

To celebrate Easter, we eat
chocolate eggs.

blossom

chocolate egg

rabbit

Easter
basket

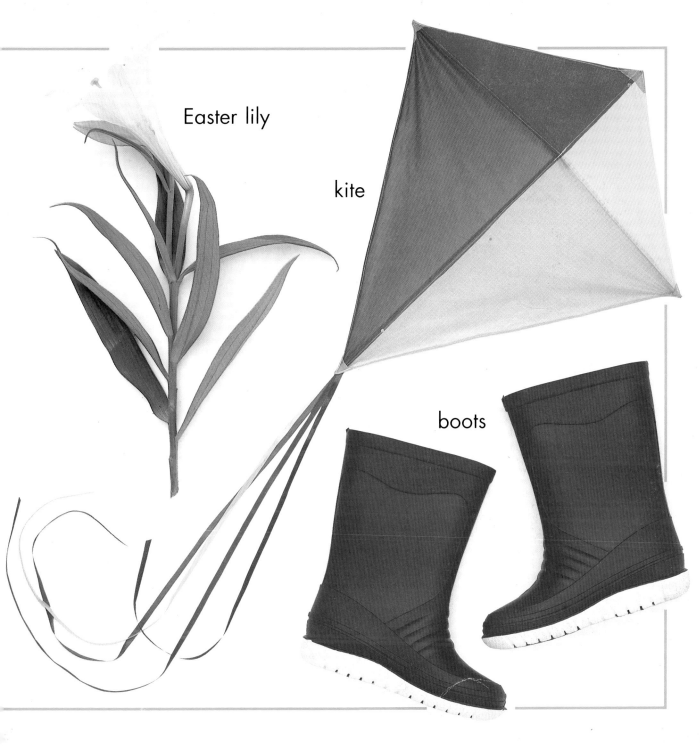

Easter lily

kite

boots

bee

Summer

In summer it's fun to have a picnic.

roses

ice
pop

butterflies

ivy

sun hat

leaves

thermos

forks and
knives

tablecloth

cheese

tomatoes

strawberries

bread

plate

picnic
basket

cup

napkins

fruit

Summer

Summer days are hot and sunny.

seaweed

sunglasses

flip-flops

bucket of
sand

shell

shovel

shells, sand,
and starfish

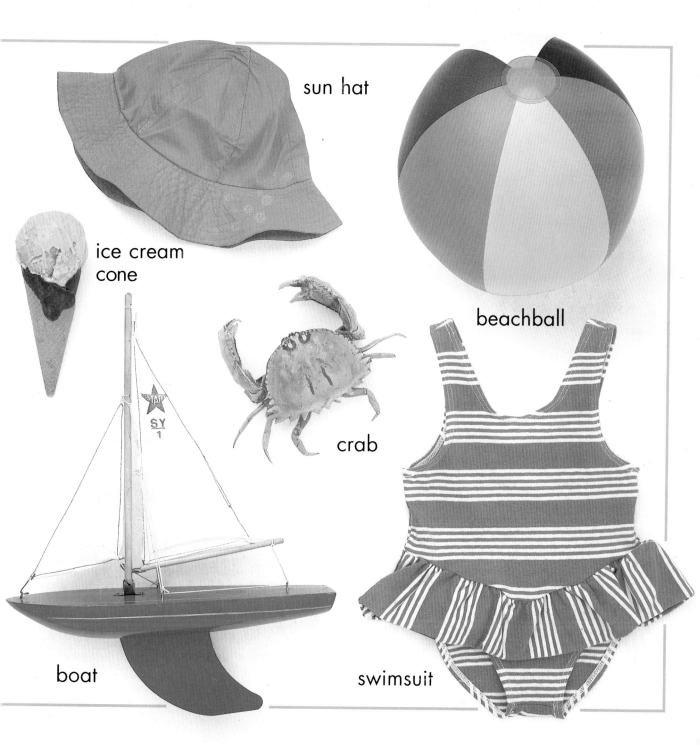

sun hat

beachball

ice cream cone

crab

boat

swimsuit

Fall

In fall the leaves change colors.

gourds

wheat

basket of apples

leaves

berries

rose hips

schoolbag

leaves

berries

Fall

It's fun to make a
jack-o'-lantern for Halloween.

flowers

sweater

nutcracker

chestnuts

acorns

nuts

squirrel

jack-o'-lantern

rake

Winter

Winter days are cold and frosty.

pine cones

scarf

hot
chocolate

holly

snowballs

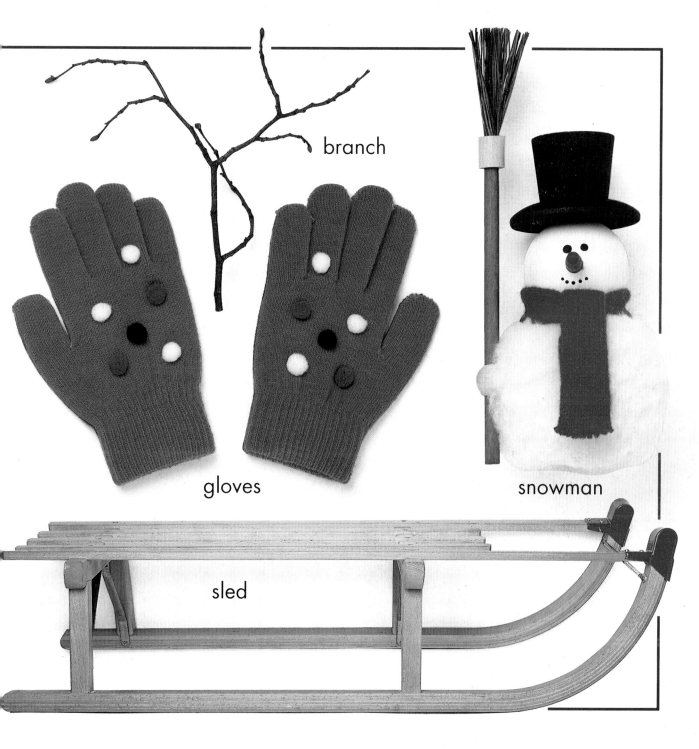

branch

gloves

snowman

sled

Winter

On December 25 we say,
"Merry Christmas!"

Christmas balls

ribbon

angel

cards

candle

Santa Claus

wreath

bells

presents

Christmas
tree

stocking

pine branch